Jobsite Mileage Log

A Small Business Mileage Logbook for Work Trucks, Pickups & Contractors - Track Trips for Tax Time

A. Herrick

Herrick, A.

Jobsite Mileage Log: A Small Business Mileage Logbook for Work Trucks, Pickups & Contractors - Track Trips for Tax Time

First edition
Christiansted, US Virgin Islands: A. Herrick, 2026

VIII, 119 pages, 6 by 9 inches

Business | Accounting Records and Bookkeeping | Mileage|

ISBN 978-1-960427-66-3

LCCN – Not assigned

657.2

A. Herrick's books may be purchased in bulk for premiums, groups, educational, business or sales promotional use. For information, please write to: Amy@AmyRoseHerrick.com.

Disclaimer: The information and/or documents contained in this book do not constitute legal or financial advice and should never be used without first consulting with other professionals to determine what may be best for your individual needs. The publisher and the author do not make any guarantee or other promise as to any results that may be obtained from using the content of this book. The publisher and the author make no guarantees concerning the level of success you may experience by following the advice and strategies contained in this book, and you accept the risk that results will differ for everyone. Although the publisher and the author have made every effort to ensure that the information in this book was correct at press time, and while this publication is designed to provide accurate information in regard to the subject matter covered, the publisher and the author assume no responsibility for errors, inaccuracies, omissions, or any other inconsistencies herein and hereby disclaim any liability to any party for any loss, damage, or disruption caused by errors or omissions, whether such errors or omissions result from negligence, accident, or any other cause. If any names are used in any illustration, they have been changed to protect the privacy of the individual.

Jobsite Mileage Log

Not for OTR/CDL/IFTA use.

Vehicle Make / Model / Year _______________________

VIN (Vehicle Identification Number)

____ (OPTIONAL)

License Plate Number _____________________ (OPTIONAL)

Business Name _________________________________

Owner Name ___________________________________

Contact Number / Email _________________________

Purchase Date _________________________________

Date placed in service __________________________

Purchase Price ________________________________

Beginning Odometer ___________________Date________

Ending Odometer _____________________Date________

Primary Business Use (check all that apply):
☐ Jobsite travel ☐ Service calls ☐ Supplies pickup
☐ Client visits ☐ Deliveries ☐ Equipment hauling
☐ Other:_______________________________

Vehicle Change

What if you change Vehicles mid-year? You will need this page to record it:

Selling price of the prior vehicle $________________________

Date of sale____

New Vehicle Make / Model / Year ___________________________

VIN (Vehicle Identification Number)

____ (OPTIONAL)

License Plate Number ___________________________ (OPTIONAL)

Business Name ____

Owner Name ____

Contact Number / Email ____________________________________

Purchase Date ____

Date placed in service _____________________________________

Purchase Price ____

Beginning Odometer _______________________________Date__________

Ending Odometer _________________________________Date__________

Primary Business Use (check all that apply):
☐ Jobsite travel ☐ Service calls ☐ Supplies pickup

V

☐ Client visits ☐ Deliveries ☐ Equipment hauling
☐ Other: _______________________________

Primary Business Use (check all that apply):
☐ Jobsite travel ☐ Service calls ☐ Supplies pickup
☐ Client visits ☐ Deliveries ☐ Equipment hauling
☐ Other: _______________________________

Content

Quick Start

JOBSITE MILEAGE LOG

This edition is built for contractors, trades, service pros, and anyone who lives on the road between estimates, jobsites, suppliers, and inspections.

Your #1 rule: Always write the **jobsite or project purpose** so the trip makes sense later.

Capacity: Includes space for **1,000+ trip entries.**

Keep it simple: record the trip + purpose + mileage.

This logbook is designed to help you maintain IRS-style records for business mileage. For each trip, record the date, starting and ending odometer readings, total miles driven, and the business purpose.

Add parking and tolls when applicable.

Complete each entry on the day the trip occurs.

At the end of every month, use the Monthly Summary pages to confirm totals and verify your odometer readings.

Keeping accurate, timely records ensures you have everything you need for year-end reporting or tax preparation.

Disclaimer

This logbook is a recordkeeping tool. It is **not** legal or tax advice. If you're unsure how to classify trips for your situation, consult a qualified tax professional

Purpose Phrases for Contractors (Use These)

- Estimate / bid visit
- Jobsite visit — work performed
- Jobsite inspection / walkthrough
- Materials pickup — (store name)
- Tool pickup / repair
- Dumpster / disposal run
- Subcontractor meeting
- Permit office / inspection scheduling
- Customer meeting — change order
- Final walkthrough / punch list
- Emergency service call
- Equipment rental pickup/return

Tip: Add the project name or initials at the end: "Materials pickup — Home Depot — Smith kitchen."

Tax year: _______________

Standard mileage rate (check IRS):

Business ______ **per mile**

Medical ______ **per mile**

Charity ______ **per mile**

Load / Haul Notes (Optional)

This is **not** a CDL/IFTA log. These pages exist for real-life context.

Date   Trip Purpose   What Was Hauled (brief) Notes

Project Codes & Quick Reference

If you track multiple jobs, use a simple code to
save time.

Project Code   Description

____

____

____

____

____

____

____

____

____

Jobsite Roster

Project / Customer	Address / Area	Notes (gate code, contact, etc.)

Jobsite Roster

Project / Customer	Address / Area	Notes (gate code, contact, etc.)

Jobsite Roster

Project / Customer	Address / Area	Notes (gate code, contact, etc.)

Jobsite Roster

Project / Customer	Address / Area	Notes (gate code, contact, etc.)

Jobsite Roster

Project / Customer	Address / Area	Notes (gate code, contact, etc.)

Extra Materials Runs Tracker

(Avoids missing extra supplies or materials needed that could be billed out to a job that would otherwise be missed.)

Date _____________ **Store**

____

Project Code _______________ **Purchase amount** $_______________

Receipt given to whom? _______________________________________

What was picked up? ____

Who picked it up? ____

Authorized by? ____

Why? ____

Bill to customer name (When applies):

____

☐ **Billed** ☐ **Not billed** ☐ **Not billable**

If company cannot bill this to a customer, why

____

Extra Materials Runs Tracker

(Avoids missing extra supplies or materials needed that could be billed out to a job that would otherwise be missed.)

Date _____________ Store

____

Project Code _____________ Purchase amount $_________________

Receipt given to whom? _________________________________

What was picked up? _____________________________________

Who picked it up? _______________________________________

Authorized by? ____

Why? ____

Bill to customer name (When applies):

____

☐ Billed ☐ Not billed ☐ Not billable

If company cannot bill this to a customer, why

____

Extra Materials Runs Tracker

(Avoids missing extra supplies or materials needed that could be billed out to a job that would otherwise be missed.)

Date _____________Store

____

Project Code _______________ Purchase amount $_________________

Receipt given to whom? ____

What was picked up? ____

Who picked it up? ____

Authorized by? ____

Why? ____

Bill to customer name (When applies):

____

☐ Billed ☐ Not billed ☐ Not billable

If company cannot bill this to a customer, why

____

Extra Materials Runs Tracker

(Avoids missing extra supplies or materials needed that could be billed out to a job that would otherwise be missed.)

Date ______________Store

____

Project Code ______________ Purchase amount $________________

Receipt given to whom? _________________________________

What was picked up? ___________________________________

Who picked it up? _____________________________________

Authorized by? _______________________________________

Why? ____

Bill to customer name (When applies):

____

☐ Billed ☐ Not billed ☐ Not billable

If company cannot bill this to a customer, why

Extra Materials Runs Tracker

(Avoids missing extra supplies or materials needed that could be billed out to a job that would otherwise be missed.)

Date _____________ **Store**

____

Project Code _____________ **Purchase amount $**_______________

Receipt given to whom? _________________________________

What was picked up? _________________________________

Who picked it up? _________________________________

Authorized by? _________________________________

Why? _________________________________

Bill to customer name (When applies):

____

☐ Billed ☐ Not billed ☐ Not billable

If company cannot bill this to a customer, why

Extra Materials Runs Tracker

(Avoids missing extra supplies or materials needed that could be billed out to a job that would otherwise be missed.)

Date _____________Store

____

Project Code _____________ Purchase amount $_______________

Receipt given to whom? _________________________________

What was picked up? ___________________________________

Who picked it up? _____________________________________

Authorized by? _______________________________________

Why? ____

Bill to customer name (When applies):

____

☐ Billed ☐ Not billed ☐ Not billable

If company cannot bill this to a customer, why

Fuel Tracker Pages (Optional)

Fuel Tracker

Date   Amount   Location   Odometer   Gallons

Fuel Tracker

Date	Amount	Location	Odometer	Gallons

Fuel Tracker

Date Amount Location Odometer Gallons

Fuel Tracker

Date	Amount	Location	Odometer	Gallons

Fuel Tracker

Date   Amount   Location   Odometer   Gallons

Service & Maintenance Log Pages (Optional)

Service & Maintenance Log

Date	Amount Vendor	Service Notes	Odometer	Warranty Period

Service & Maintenance Log

Date	Amount Vendor	Service Notes	Odometer	Warranty Period

Service & Maintenance Log

Date	Amount Vendor	Service Notes	Odometer	Warranty Period

Service & Maintenance Log

Date	Amount Vendor	Service Notes	Odometer	Warranty Period

Service & Maintenance Log

Date   Amount Vendor   Service Notes   Odometer   Warranty Period

Mixed-Use Reality Check & Log Pages

Most contractors have mixed-stop days… keep notes so the purpose is clear later.

Don't turn your mileage log into a guessing game.

What helps your records:

- Write the purpose every time
- Keep the mileage consistent
- Add notes on mixed-stop days
- Don't "estimate later" (later becomes never)

Multiple Stops Day Log

(Stops: ___) Date: __________

Start Odometer: _________ End Odometer: _________
Total Business Miles: _________

Stops / Notes:

Multiple Stops Day Log

(Stops: ___) Date: __________

Start Odometer: _________ End Odometer: _________
Total Business Miles: _________

Stops / Notes:

Multiple Stops Day Log

(Stops: ___) Date: ___________

Start Odometer: _________ End Odometer: _________
Total Business Miles: _________

Stops / Notes:

Multiple Stops Day Log

(Stops: ___) Date: ___________

Start Odometer: _________ End Odometer: _________
Total Business Miles: _________

Stops / Notes:

Multiple Stops Day Log

(Stops: ___) Date: ___________

Start Odometer: _________ End Odometer: _________
Total Business Miles: _________

Stops / Notes:

Multiple Stops Day Log

(Stops: ___) Date: ___________

Start Odometer: _________ End Odometer: _________
Total Business Miles: _________

Stops / Notes:

Multiple Stops Day Log

(Stops: ___) Date: ___________

Start Odometer: _________ End Odometer: _________
Total Business Miles: _________

Stops / Notes:

Multiple Stops Day Log

(Stops: ___) Date: ___________

Start Odometer: _________ End Odometer: _________
Total Business Miles: _________

Stops / Notes:

Multiple Stops Day Log

(Stops: ___) Date: ___________

Start Odometer: __________ End Odometer: __________
Total Business Miles: __________

Stops / Notes:

Multiple Stops Day Log

(Stops: ___) Date: ___________

Start Odometer: __________ End Odometer: __________
Total Business Miles: __________

Stops / Notes:

Multiple Stops Day Log

(Stops: ___) Date: ___________

Start Odometer: __________ End Odometer: __________
Total Business Miles: __________

Stops / Notes:

Multiple Stops Day Log

(Stops: ___) Date: ___________

Start Odometer: __________ End Odometer: __________
Total Business Miles: __________

Stops / Notes:

Multiple Stops Day Log

(Stops: ___) Date: ___________

Start Odometer: _________ End Odometer: _________
Total Business Miles: _________

Stops / Notes:

Multiple Stops Day Log

(Stops: ___) Date: ___________

Start Odometer: _________ End Odometer: _________
Total Business Miles: _________

Stops / Notes:

Multiple Stops Day Log

(Stops: ___) Date: ___________

Start Odometer: _________ End Odometer: _________
Total Business Miles: _________

Stops / Notes:

Multiple Stops Day Log

(Stops: ___) Date: ___________

Start Odometer: _________ End Odometer: _________
Total Business Miles: _________

Stops / Notes:

Multiple Stops Day Log

(Stops: ___) Date: ___________

Start Odometer: _________ End Odometer: _________
Total Business Miles: _________

Stops / Notes:

Multiple Stops Day Log

(Stops: ___) Date: ___________

Start Odometer: _________ End Odometer: _________
Total Business Miles: _________

Stops / Notes:

Multiple Stops Day Log

(Stops: ___) Date: ___________

Start Odometer: _________ End Odometer: _________
Total Business Miles: _________

Stops / Notes:

Multiple Stops Day Log

(Stops: ___) Date: ___________

Start Odometer: _________ End Odometer: _________
Total Business Miles: _________

Stops / Notes:

Multiple Stops Day Log

(Stops: ___) Date: ___________

Start Odometer: _________ End Odometer: _________
Total Business Miles: _________

Stops / Notes:

Multiple Stops Day Log

(Stops: ___) Date: ___________

Start Odometer: _________ End Odometer: _________
Total Business Miles: _________

Stops / Notes:

Multiple Stops Day Log

(Stops: ___) Date: ___________

Start Odometer: _________ End Odometer: _________
Total Business Miles: _________

Stops / Notes:

Multiple Stops Day Log

(Stops: ___) Date: ___________

Start Odometer: _________ End Odometer: _________
Total Business Miles: _________

Stops / Notes:

Multiple Stops Day Log

(Stops: ___) Date: __________

Start Odometer: _________ End Odometer: _________
Total Business Miles: _________

Stops / Notes:

Multiple Stops Day Log

(Stops: ___) Date: __________

Start Odometer: _________ End Odometer: _________
Total Business Miles: _________

Stops / Notes:

Multiple Stops Day Log

(Stops: ___) Date: ___________

Start Odometer: __________ End Odometer: __________
Total Business Miles: __________

Stops / Notes:

Multiple Stops Day Log

(Stops: ___) Date: ___________

Start Odometer: __________ End Odometer: __________
Total Business Miles: __________

Stops / Notes:

Multiple Stops Day Log

(Stops: ___) Date: ___________

Start Odometer: _________ End Odometer: _________
Total Business Miles: _________

Stops / Notes:

Multiple Stops Day Log

(Stops: ___) Date: ___________

Start Odometer: _________ End Odometer: _________
Total Business Miles: _________

Stops / Notes:

Multiple Stops Day Log

(Stops: ___) Date: ___________

Start Odometer: _________ End Odometer: _________
Total Business Miles: _________

Stops / Notes:

Multiple Stops Day Log

(Stops: ___) Date: ___________

Start Odometer: _________ End Odometer: _________
Total Business Miles: _________

Stops / Notes:

Multiple Stops Day Log

(Stops: ___) Date: ____________

Start Odometer: __________ End Odometer: __________
Total Business Miles: __________

Stops / Notes:

Multiple Stops Day Log

(Stops: ___) Date: ____________

Start Odometer: __________ End Odometer: __________
Total Business Miles: __________

Stops / Notes:

Multiple Stops Day Log

(Stops: ___) Date: ___________

Start Odometer: __________ End Odometer: __________
Total Business Miles: __________

Stops / Notes:

Multiple Stops Day Log

(Stops: ___) Date: ___________

Start Odometer: __________ End Odometer: __________
Total Business Miles: __________

Stops / Notes:

Multiple Stops Day Log

(Stops: ___) Date: ___________

Start Odometer: _________ End Odometer: _________
Total Business Miles: _________

Stops / Notes:

Multiple Stops Day Log

(Stops: ___) Date: ___________

Start Odometer: _________ End Odometer: _________
Total Business Miles: _________

Stops / Notes:

Multiple Stops Day Log

(Stops: ___) Date: ___________

Start Odometer: _________ End Odometer: _________
Total Business Miles: _________

Stops / Notes:

Multiple Stops Day Log

(Stops: ___) Date: ___________

Start Odometer: _________ End Odometer: _________
Total Business Miles: _________

Stops / Notes:

Multiple Stops Day Log

(Stops: ___) Date: ___________

Start Odometer: __________ End Odometer: __________
Total Business Miles: __________

Stops / Notes:

Multiple Stops Day Log

(Stops: ___) Date: ___________

Start Odometer: __________ End Odometer: __________
Total Business Miles: __________

Stops / Notes:

Multiple Stops Day Log

(Stops: ___) Date: ___________

Start Odometer: _________ End Odometer: _________
Total Business Miles: _________

Stops / Notes:

Multiple Stops Day Log

(Stops: ___) Date: ___________

Start Odometer: _________ End Odometer: _________
Total Business Miles: _________

Stops / Notes:

Multiple Stops Day Log

(Stops: ___) Date: ___________

Start Odometer: _________ End Odometer: _________
Total Business Miles: _________

Stops / Notes:

Multiple Stops Day Log

(Stops: ___) Date: ___________

Start Odometer: _________ End Odometer: _________
Total Business Miles: _________

Stops / Notes:

Multiple Stops Day Log

(Stops: ___) Date: ____________

Start Odometer: ___________ End Odometer: ___________
Total Business Miles: ___________

Stops / Notes:

Multiple Stops Day Log

(Stops: ___) Date: ____________

Start Odometer: ___________ End Odometer: ___________
Total Business Miles: ___________

Stops / Notes:

Multiple Stops Day Log

(Stops: ___) Date: ___________

Start Odometer: _________ End Odometer: _________
Total Business Miles: _________

Stops / Notes:

Multiple Stops Day Log

(Stops: ___) Date: ___________

Start Odometer: _________ End Odometer: _________
Total Business Miles: _________

Stops / Notes:

Jobsite Mileage Log

Date	Starting Odometer	Ending Odometer	Total Miles	Purpose of Trip	Parking & Tolls Cost

Total

Jobsite Mileage Log

Date	Starting Odometer	Ending Odometer	Total Miles	Purpose of Trip	Parking & Tolls Cost

Total

Jobsite Mileage Log

Date	Starting Odometer	Ending Odometer	Total Miles	Purpose of Trip	Parking & Tolls Cost

Total

Jobsite Mileage Log

Date	Starting Odometer	Ending Odometer	Total Miles	Purpose of Trip	Parking & Tolls Cost
					Total

Jobsite Mileage Log

Date	Starting Odometer	Ending Odometer	Total Miles	Purpose of Trip	Parking & Tolls Cost

Total

Jobsite Mileage Log

Date	Starting Odometer	Ending Odometer	Total Miles	Purpose of Trip	Parking & Tolls Cost
			Total		

Jobsite Mileage Log

Date	Starting Odometer	Ending Odometer	Total Miles	Purpose of Trip	Parking & Tolls Cost
				Total	

Jobsite Mileage Log

Date	Starting Odometer	Ending Odometer	Total Miles	Purpose of Trip	Parking & Tolls Cost

Total

Jobsite Mileage Log

Date	Starting Odometer	Ending Odometer	Total Miles	Purpose of Trip	Parking & Tolls Cost
			Total		

Jobsite Mileage Log Jobsite Mileage Log

Date	Starting Odometer	Ending Odometer	Total Miles	Purpose of Trip	Parking & Tolls Cost

Total

Jobsite Mileage Log

Date	Starting Odometer	Ending Odometer	Total Miles	Purpose of Trip	Parking & Tolls Cost

Total

Jobsite Mileage Log

Date	Starting Odometer	Ending Odometer	Total Miles	Purpose of Trip	Parking & Tolls Cost

Total

Jobsite Mileage Log

Date	Starting Odometer	Ending Odometer	Total Miles	Purpose of Trip	Parking & Tolls Cost

Total

Jobsite Mileage Log

Date	Starting Odometer	Ending Odometer	Total Miles	Purpose of Trip	Parking & Tolls Cost

Total

Jobsite Mileage Log

Date	Starting Odometer	Ending Odometer	Total Miles	Purpose of Trip	Parking & Tolls Cost

Total

Jobsite Mileage Log

Date	Starting Odometer	Ending Odometer	Total Miles	Purpose of Trip	Parking & Tolls Cost

Total

Jobsite Mileage Log

Date	Starting Odometer	Ending Odometer	Total Miles	Purpose of Trip	Parking & Tolls Cost

Total

Jobsite Mileage Log

Date	Starting Odometer	Ending Odometer	Total Miles	Purpose of Trip	Parking & Tolls Cost
				Total	

Jobsite Mileage Log

Date	Starting Odometer	Ending Odometer	Total Miles	Purpose of Trip	Parking & Tolls Cost

Total

Jobsite Mileage Log

Date	Starting Odometer	Ending Odometer	Total Miles	Purpose of Trip	Parking & Tolls Cost
			Total		

Jobsite Mileage Log

Date	Starting Odometer	Ending Odometer	Total Miles	Purpose of Trip	Parking & Tolls Cost

Total

Jobsite Mileage Log

Date	Starting Odometer	Ending Odometer	Total Miles	Purpose of Trip	Parking & Tolls Cost
				Total	

Jobsite Mileage Log

Date	Starting Odometer	Ending Odometer	Total Miles	Purpose of Trip	Parking & Tolls Cost

Total

Jobsite Mileage Log

Date	Starting Odometer	Ending Odometer	Total Miles	Purpose of Trip	Parking & Tolls Cost
			Total		

Jobsite Mileage Log

Date	Starting Odometer	Ending Odometer	Total Miles	Purpose of Trip	Parking & Tolls Cost

Total

Jobsite Mileage Log

Date	Starting Odometer	Ending Odometer	Total Miles	Purpose of Trip	Parking & Tolls Cost

Total

Jobsite Mileage Log

Date	Starting Odometer	Ending Odometer	Total Miles	Purpose of Trip	Parking & Tolls Cost

Total

Jobsite Mileage Log

Date	Starting Odometer	Ending Odometer	Total Miles	Purpose of Trip	Parking & Tolls Cost

Total

Jobsite Mileage Log

Date	Starting Odometer	Ending Odometer	Total Miles	Purpose of Trip	Parking & Tolls Cost

Total

Jobsite Mileage Log

Date	Starting Odometer	Ending Odometer	Total Miles	Purpose of Trip	Parking & Tolls Cost

Total

Jobsite Mileage Log

Date	Starting Odometer	Ending Odometer	Total Miles	Purpose of Trip	Parking & Tolls Cost

Total

Jobsite Mileage Log

Date	Starting Odometer	Ending Odometer	Total Miles	Purpose of Trip	Parking & Tolls Cost

Total

Jobsite Mileage Log

Date	Starting Odometer	Ending Odometer	Total Miles	Purpose of Trip	Parking & Tolls Cost
				Total	

Jobsite Mileage Log

Date	Starting Odometer	Ending Odometer	Total Miles	Purpose of Trip	Parking & Tolls Cost
				Total	

Jobsite Mileage Log

Date	Starting Odometer	Ending Odometer	Total Miles	Purpose of Trip	Parking & Tolls Cost
					Total

Jobsite Mileage Log

Date	Starting Odometer	Ending Odometer	Total Miles	Purpose of Trip	Parking & Tolls Cost

Total

Jobsite Mileage Log

Date	Starting Odometer	Ending Odometer	Total Miles	Purpose of Trip	Parking & Tolls Cost
				Total	

Jobsite Mileage Log

Date	Starting Odometer	Ending Odometer	Total Miles	Purpose of Trip	Parking & Tolls Cost

Total

Jobsite Mileage Log

Date	Starting Odometer	Ending Odometer	Total Miles	Purpose of Trip	Parking & Tolls Cost
			Total		

Jobsite Mileage Log

Date	Starting Odometer	Ending Odometer	Total Miles	Purpose of Trip	Parking & Tolls Cost

Total

Jobsite Mileage Log

Date	Starting Odometer	Ending Odometer	Total Miles	Purpose of Trip	Parking & Tolls Cost

Total

Jobsite Mileage Log

Date	Starting Odometer	Ending Odometer	Total Miles	Purpose of Trip	Parking & Tolls Cost

Total

Jobsite Mileage Log

Date	Starting Odometer	Ending Odometer	Total Miles	Purpose of Trip	Parking & Tolls Cost

Total

Jobsite Mileage Log

Date	Starting Odometer	Ending Odometer	Total Miles	Purpose of Trip	Parking & Tolls Cost

Total

Monthly Summary Pages
(RECOMMENDED)

January Monthly Summary

Monthly Mileage Audit-Ready Checklist

☐ All trip purposes clearly labeled

☐ Monthly totals completed

☐ Odometer start and end recorded

Odometer Start _______________________________________

Odometer End _______________________________________

Total Miles _______________________________________

Total Miles – Business Miles = Personal Miles____________

Business Miles _______________________________________

Parking/Tolls $_______________________________________

February Monthly Summary

Monthly Mileage Audit-Ready Checklist

☐ All trip purposes clearly labeled

☐ Monthly totals completed

☐ Odometer start and end recorded

Odometer Start ___________________________________

Odometer End ___________________________________

Total Miles ___________________________________

Total Miles – Business Miles = Personal Miles___________

Business Miles _________________________________

Parking/Tolls $________________________________

March Monthly Summary

Monthly Mileage Audit-Ready Checklist

☐ All trip purposes clearly labeled

☐ Monthly totals completed

☐ Odometer start and end recorded

Odometer Start   ____

Odometer End   ____

Total Miles   ____

Total Miles – Business Miles = Personal Miles__________

Business Miles   ____

Parking/Tolls $____

April Monthly Summary

Monthly Mileage Audit-Ready Checklist

☐ All trip purposes clearly labeled

☐ Monthly totals completed

☐ Odometer start and end recorded

Odometer Start   _________________________________

Odometer End   _________________________________

Total Miles   _________________________________

Total Miles – Business Miles = Personal Miles___________

Business Miles   _________________________________

Parking/Tolls $_______________________________

May Monthly Summary

Monthly Mileage Audit-Ready Checklist

☐ All trip purposes clearly labeled

☐ Monthly totals completed

☐ Odometer start and end recorded

Odometer Start _________________________________

Odometer End _________________________________

Total Miles _________________________________

Total Miles – Business Miles = Personal Miles___________

Business Miles _________________________________

Parking/Tolls $_______________________________

June Monthly Summary

Monthly Mileage Audit-Ready Checklist

☐ All trip purposes clearly labeled

☐ Monthly totals completed

☐ Odometer start and end recorded

Odometer Start ______________________________

Odometer End ______________________________

Total Miles ______________________________

Total Miles – Business Miles = Personal Miles____________

Business Miles ______________________________

Parking/Tolls $______________________________

July Monthly Summary

Monthly Mileage Audit-Ready Checklist

☐ All trip purposes clearly labeled

☐ Monthly totals completed

☐ Odometer start and end recorded

Odometer Start ____

Odometer End ____

Total Miles ____

Total Miles – Business Miles = Personal Miles____________

Business Miles ____

Parking/Tolls $____

August Monthly Summary

Monthly Mileage Audit-Ready Checklist

☐ All trip purposes clearly labeled

☐ Monthly totals completed

☐ Odometer start and end recorded

Odometer Start _______________________________

Odometer End _______________________________

Total Miles _______________________________

Total Miles – Business Miles = Personal Miles____________

Business Miles _______________________________

Parking/Tolls $_______________________________

September Monthly Summary

Monthly Mileage Audit-Ready Checklist

☐ All trip purposes clearly labeled

☐ Monthly totals completed

☐ Odometer start and end recorded

Odometer Start _______________________________________

Odometer End _______________________________________

Total Miles _______________________________________

Total Miles – Business Miles = Personal Miles____________

Business Miles _______________________________________

Parking/Tolls $_______________________________________

October Monthly Summary

Monthly Mileage Audit-Ready Checklist

☐ All trip purposes clearly labeled

☐ Monthly totals completed

☐ Odometer start and end recorded

Odometer Start _______________________________________

Odometer End _______________________________________

Total Miles _______________________________________

Total Miles – Business Miles = Personal Miles____________

Business Miles _______________________________________

Parking/Tolls $_______________________________________

November Monthly Summary

Monthly Mileage Audit-Ready Checklist

☐ All trip purposes clearly labeled

☐ Monthly totals completed

☐ Odometer start and end recorded

Odometer Start _______________________________________

Odometer End _______________________________________

Total Miles _______________________________________

Total Miles – Business Miles = Personal Miles____________

Business Miles _______________________________________

Parking/Tolls $_______________________________________

December Monthly Summary

Monthly Mileage Audit-Ready Checklist

☐ All trip purposes clearly labeled

☐ Monthly totals completed

☐ Odometer start and end recorded

Odometer Start   ______________________________

Odometer End   ______________________________

Total Miles   ______________________________

Total Miles – Business Miles = Personal Miles__________

Business Miles   ______________________________

Parking/Tolls $______________________________

Tax-Time Contractor Checklist

- ☐ Jobsite roster pages are filled out (or most used jobsites are listed)

- ☐ Trips show jobsite/purpose (estimate, materials, service call, etc.)

- ☐ Multiple stop days have notes

- ☐ Monthly totals are completed (optional but helpful)

- ☐ You did not mix multiple vehicles into one log unless clearly labeled

Year-End Preparation Checklist

☐ All logs total per month

    1. ☐ Beginning and ending Odometer readings confirmed

    2. ☐ Data shared with your preparer

<u>NOTE FROM THE AUTHOR</u>: Thank you for using this job site mileage log designed for contractors and work-truck travel.

If you found value in this book, please take a minute to leave a review.

Annual Summary

Odometer Start ______________________

Odometer End ______________________

Total Miles ______________________

Business Miles ______________________

Personal Miles ______________________

Parking/Tolls $______________________

Fuel $______________________

9 781960 427663